Jemimah Hendrick practises in all areas of family law including public and private law children, financial relief and TLATA as well as undertaking work in the Court of Protection.

Jemimah appears for local authorities, parents, children's guardians and 'P' and has appeared in cases that have included non-accidental injuries, international abduction, committals, sexual abuse, cryptic pregnancies, forced marriage, FGM and issues of reporting cases and transparency. She has a particular interest in the 'cross over cases' for young people between the family courts and the Court of Protection and appears regularly in the DOLs court.

Amelia Culverwell practises across all areas of children law including public and private. She represents local authorities, parents and children's guardians and has been instructed in a wide variety of cases including those with allegations of sexual abuse, non-accidental injuries, forced marriage, and alienating behaviours. Amelia has a particular interest in representing vulnerable clients, including those who lack capacity. She regularly appears in the family court, the Court of Protection and the DOLs court.

A Practical Guide to Deprivation of Liberty Orders for Children and Young People in the Family Court and Court of Protection

A Practical Guide to Deprivation of Liberty Orders for Children and Young People in the Family Court and Court of Protection

Jemimah Hendrick
Barrister, New Court Chambers

Amelia Culverwell
Barrister, New Court Chambers

Law Brief Publishing

Published 2026 by Law Brief Publishing, an imprint of Law Brief Publishing Ltd
30 The Parks
Minehead
Somerset
TA24 8BT

www.lawbriefpublishing.com

Paperback: 978-1-918241-25-9

PREFACE

The number of Deprivation of Liberty order applications is on the rise, especially those in relation to children and young people. There is often confusion as to the right place to issue (whether that should be under the inherent jurisdiction in the family court or, in the Court of Protection), the relevant tests and the appropriate steps to take in these 'cross over' cases.

This book focuses specifically on applications for Deprivation of Liberty Orders in relation to those children and young people aged 17 years old and under and sets out the legal and practical matters that will need to be considered to ensure the right application is made in the right court, in the right way.

Practitioners will find within advice on how to determine which jurisdiction to issue under, what the relevant tests are in each jurisdiction, what is relevant to be considered by the court when making these orders and the practical steps that need to be taken. There is also a break-down of the process that practitioners can expect once an application has been issued in either jurisdiction. There is also advice on the types of restrictions that do not require authorisation with a Deprivation of Liberty order.

The law is correct as at 2 February 2026.

Jemimah Hendrick
Amelia Culverwell
February 2026

CONTENTS

CHAPTER ONE

WHAT IS A DEPRIVATION OF LIBERTY ORDER?

This chapter sets out:

1. The leading authority on deprivation of liberty order
2. The application of Article 5
3. Essential character of the deprivation of liberty orders
    a. The objective component
    b. The subjective component
        i. If under 16
        ii. If 16 or 17
    c. The attribution of responsibility to the state
    d. Irrelevant considerations

The leading authority

The very first question you must ask yourself when you are considering whether a DOLs application may be necessary, is "does this care plan amount to a deprivation of liberty for the child or young person?". There is now an established test for this question set out by the relevant jurisprudence.

The leading precedent cases are *P v Cheshire West and Chester Council and another; P and another v Surrey County Council* [2014] 2 All ER 585, where the Supreme Court (Lord Neuberger, Lady Hale (as she then was) and Lord Sumption) considered whether living arrangements for three mentally incapacitated adults amounted to a deprivation of their Article 5 rights, and therefore required authorisation under the deprivation of liberty safeguards. Lady Hale delivered the leading judgment, setting out "that human rights are for everyone, including the most disabled members of our community, and that those rights include the same right to liberty as has everyone else' [1]. At [2]-[10], Lady Hale sets out a comprehensive history of the deprivation of liberty safeguards and at [19]-[32], sets out what is meant by a deprivation of liberty. In summary, the UK courts turn to the jurisprudence of Strasbourg.

Specific facts of P v Cheshire West

In *P v Cheshire West and Chester Council and another*, P was an adult who had cerebral palsy and Down's Syndrome and required 24-hour care to meet his personal care needs. He had lived with his mother until her deteriorating health led the local authority to apply for orders that it was in his best interests to move to local authority accommodation where he was supported by staff at all times (two members during the day, one overnight). Staff supported him to attend a day centre, to see his mother, and to go the pub and the shops. He required staff support with all aspects of his care both in and out of his accommodation and they also had to manage some of his challenging behaviours. At first instance in COP, the judge concluded that he was under the full control of the staff and could not do anything without their support and thus P was clearly having his liberty deprived. The judge determined that it was in his best interests for those restrictions to continue. On appeal, the Court of Appeal ([2011] EWCA Civ1257) applied a "relative normality" test and compared P's life to that which those with similar difficulties might expect to lead, rather than that which he had led when he resided with his mother.

In *P and another v Surrey County Council* [2010] EWHC 785 (Fam) two sisters had been subject to care proceedings when aged 16 and 15. The care proceedings then transferred to COP when the sisters were 17 and 16. They both had learning disabilities, with the eldest (MIG) having more significant needs than the youngest (MEG). MIG had communication and understanding difficulties with no danger awareness, for example she required help crossing the road. MEG had better communication and understanding but she had autistic traits and challenging behaviours. MIG was 18 at the time of the case and was living with a foster mother who provided significant support to her across all areas of her life. She was not receiving any medication. She attended an education unit during term time and her foster mother took her on trips and holidays. She had no interest in leaving the foster home but her foster carer would stop her should she try to do so. MEG was 17 and had been living with a different foster carer who struggled to manage her complex behaviours and so she moved to a residential NHS facility for adolescents with learning difficulties and complex needs. MEG occasionally required physical restraint and was given tranquilising medication. She required continuous supervision and control in order for her care needs to be met. She also showed no interest in going out of the placement and so did not have to be prevented from doing so. She attended the same education unit as MIG although had a fuller social life than MIG. Whilst both sisters had high levels of need, they were differing and required different types of support and restrictions to meet their respective needs. The judge at first instance in COP held that the living arrangements for both were in their best interests and so were not a deprivation of liberty, a decision which was upheld by the Court of Appeal ([2011] EWCA Civ 190). Wilson LJ, giving the lead judgment, stressed the "relative normality" of the sisters' lives compared to that which they would have at home with their family. Smith LJ considered that their previous arrangements were irrelevant but 'what may be a deprivation of liberty for one person may not be for another' (at [40]).

The application of Article 5

The Supreme Court, in these two cases, identified that the first and most fundamental question in considering the appeals was 'whether the concept of physical liberty protected by Article 5 is the same for everyone, regardless of whether or not they are mentally or physically disabled?' and noted the differing approach taken by the lower-level court. It is clear from the Strasbourg jurisprudence that a person may be deprived of his liberty without knowing it [35] and 'the comparative benevolence of the living arrangements with which we are concerned blind us to their essential character if indeed that constitutes a deprivation of liberty' [35]. Lady Hale emphasised the universal character of human rights, and that they are to be guaranteed to everyone; people with disabilities, both physical and mental, have the same human rights as the rest of the human race [44]. Whilst their rights may need to limited or restricted due to their disabilities, the starting point is the same. Therefore, to be deprived of that physical liberty to go where you want must be the same for everyone.

Importantly, the purpose of any confinement, which may well be to a person's benefit, is not relevant to whether or not there is a deprivation of their liberty [42]. The fact that their restricted living arrangements are comfortable and make their life enjoyable, make no difference. As Lady Hale stated and is oft-cited; "*A gilded cage is still a cage*" [46].

The essential character of a deprivation of liberty

The second question that flowed was then 'what is the essential character of a deprivation of liberty?'. Strasbourg jurisprudence establishes three components that needs to be considered when assessing the character of a deprivation of liberty:

1. The objective component – which is confinement in a particular restricted place for a not negligible length of time.

2. The subjective component – which is lack of valid consent

3. The attribution of responsibility for the deprivation to the state.

These have created the foundation of the test for assessing whether or not a DOLs order is required and should be the questions you ask when considering if an application for a DOLs order needs to be made. It is important to note that this test is the same whether you are making your application under the Inherent Jurisdiction or the court of protection.

The Objective Component

The question to ask is whether the person is under continuous supervision and control. From a practitioner's perspective, indicators you should look for are:

1. High level of supervision e.g. 1:1

2. Locked interior and/or exterior doors and/or windows

3. Not being allowed out of the placement without supervision

4. If they left the unit, would they be returned i.e. would the police be called

5. Physical restraint

Age can make a significant difference in assessing whether there is a deprivation, for example a 12-year-old and a 16-year-old would have very different restrictions placed on them; a 12-year-old would not have the same level of freedom as a 16 year old.

The Subjective Component

The next question to consider is whether the child or young person can consent to the deprivation. There may be a consenting parent. However, there are a number of factors to consider which will affect whether this is sufficient for the purposes of authorising a deprivation of liberty of a child or young person.

If under 16:

1. Gives their own consent:

    - If the child is under 16 *and* Gillick competent (please see below for further information on Gillick competence) then the child can consent.

    - You must also consider whether the child would withdraw their consent at the time when the restrictions were being put in place. If they are likely to do so, then this may be sufficient for it to be argued that their consent cannot be relied upon; they need to give continuous consent to the deprivation.

- If a child is Gillick competent, gives their consent to the restriction and would not withdraw their consent, then the arrangements will not require court authorisation. However, this would be unusual in practice.

2. Parent(s) consent:

- Parent(s) can consent if the child is not Gillick competent and is under 16.

- A practitioner must be sure that there are no concerns about the parent(s) own capacity to give valid consent.

- In circumstances where a parent can give valid consent to the restrictions, the arrangements would be regulated under s20 Children Act 1989.

- A corporate parent cannot give consent, regardless of whether it holds an ICO or a final care order for a child or young person (para 18 *D (A Child)* [2020] 2 All ER 399).

A note on Gillick competence

A child under 16 is assumed not to have capacity until proven otherwise. *Gillick Competence* is the test for assessing legal capacity in children under the age of 16 years, and was established in *Gillick v West Norfolk and Wisbech Area Health Authority* (1985) 2 A11 ER 402. Children who are Gillick competent are deemed to be capable of giving valid consent to medical treatment.

Practitioners should also consider whether a child is Gillick Competent to consent to other decisions such as a deprivation of liberty. The factors to be considered when assessing whether a child is Gillick competent include:

- child's age, maturity (physical and mental) and intellect
- do they understand the problem or issue, and what it involves?
- do they understand the risks, implications and any consequences, that may arise from their decision?
- do they understand the advantages and disadvantages of the issue they face?
- do they understand any advice or information they have been given?
- do they understand any alternative options (if available)?
- can they articulate a rationale around their reasoning and decision making?

A note on parental consent

In *QX (Parental Consent for Deprivation of liberty: Children under 16)* [2025] EWHC 745 (Fam), HHJ Burrows sitting as a High Court Judge, considered the circumstances in which a person with parental responsibility can consent to DOLs. The local authority had issued applications for a care order and DOLs for QX, who was autistic with severe learning disabilities. The local authority subsequently withdrew both its applications on the basis of parental consent subsequently being given. The authorities are clear that a person with parental responsibility does not exercise substituted consent, but that the right to consent to a deprivation of liberty falls within the scope of exercising parental responsibility. Under the age of 16, children are still of an age when it would be normal for decisions to be made by a parent, even if that decision conflicted with the child's wishes.

HHJ Burrows considered the line of authority on the exercise of parental to consent to a deprivation of liberty and summarised that "*provided the exercise of parental responsibility is for the interest of the child, then it is within the zone of parental responsibility; if it is not, then it is without that zone.*" [58]. HHJ Burrows recognised that QX's parents knew best and were freely able to act in his best interests. As such, neither a care order nor DOLs were necessary. HHJ Burrows acknowledges that as a result of his decision, an identical case to QX would not now result in the need for the local authority to issue proceedings. This would leave parents and local authorities to embark on the challenge of identifying appropriate placements and arrangements for children with complex needs without judicial involvement or scrutiny. In particular, this would leave parents to make *"an agonising decision not only whether to part with their child, but also to hand that child over into an uncertain regime of intense restrictions, often with the need to change placements on a regular basis."*[67]. As such, HHJ Burrows advises local authorities to err on the side of caution and issue proceedings if there is a possibility that parents may become overwhelmed by the decision-making process or change their minds for various reasons, and thus withdraw their consent.

<u>If 16 or 17:</u>

1. Gives their own consent:

    - Valid consent ('valid' meaning that they have capacity to consent) is effective as if he/she were of full age

2. Parent(s) consent:

    - A parent (including the local authority as a corporate parent) cannot consent for a child or young person who is aged 16 or over

A summary of the law in relation to the distinction between the authority of parental consent depending on a child's age is set out by Keehan J at [38]-[39] of *Re D (A Child) (Deprivation of liberty)* [2015] EWHC 922 (Fam)).

> *36. I have been referred to the provisions of s131 MHA 1983 which states:*
>
> *131 Informal admission of patients.*
>
> *(1) Nothing in this Act shall be construed as preventing a patient who requires treatment for mental disorder from being admitted to any hospital or [registered, order or direction rendering him liable to be detained under this Act, or from remaining in any hospital or [registered establishment] in pursuance of such arrangements after he has ceased to be so liable to be detained.*
>
> *[(2) Subsections (3) and (4) below apply in the case of a patient aged 16 or 17 years who has capacity to consent to the making of such arrangements as are mentioned in subsection (1) above.*
>
> *(3) If the patient consents to the making of the arrangements, they may be made, carried out and determined on the basis of that consent even though there are one or more persons who have parental responsibility for him.*

(4) If the patient does not consent to the making of the arrangements, they may not be made, carried out or determined on the basis of the consent of a person who has parental responsibility for him.

(5) In this section—

(a) the reference to a patient who has capacity is to be read in accordance with the Mental Capacity Act 2005; and

(b) "parental responsibility" has the same meaning as in the Children Act 1989.]

37. *Further s8 FLRA 1969 provides that:*

s8(1) The consent of a minor who has attained the age of sixteen years to any surgical, medical or dental treatment which, in the absence of consent, would constitute a trespass to his person, shall be as effective as it would be if he were of full age; and where a minor has by virtue of this section given an effective consent to any treatment it shall not be necessary to obtain any consent for it from his parent or guardian.

38. *These provisions are just two examples of where Parliament has chosen, in a number of areas, to draw a distinction between a child and a young person who has yet to achieve his/her majority but who has attained the age of 16 or 17. Thus the legal authority of a parent to consent to the detention or treatment of a 16 or 17 year old is severely curtailed, if not removed.*

Attribution of responsibility to the state

The question to be asked here is whether the local authority is providing the restriction and the deprivation. If a DOLs application is being contemplated, it is highly likely that the local authority is providing the restrictions on the young person or child. This component will generally always be satisfied in family court or COP proceedings.

Irrelevant factors

For completeness' sake, please note the following factors which were identified as being irrelevant in considering whether there is a deprivation of liberty (at [50] of *P v Cheshire West*):

a. The child's compliance or lack of objection

b. Relative normality of the placement (whatever it may be compared to)

c. Reason or purpose behind a particular placement

In a pair of recent cases (*Peterborough City Council v a Mother and a Father* [2024] EWHC 493 *(Fam) and Rochdale Borough Council v V [*2025] EWHC 200 (Fam)*)* it was held that such was the mental and physical disability of the child, that <u>it</u> deprived them of their liberty and not any "restrictions" that were put in place by the state or parents to keep them safe. However, in QX HHJ Burrows concluded that these authorities "*appear to be plainly wrong*" [41].

> "*Consequently, a person, subject to a care plan that requires them to reside in a particular place and be under constant supervision and control and are not free to leave, whether or not their physical or*

> *mental capabilities prevent them from leaving, is deprived of his/her liberty, absent their consent.*" [44]

HHJ Burrows confirmed that the correct test to be applied remains that set out in *Cheshire West.*

Summary: Everyone has the same right to liberty, regardless of any disability and consequent need for deprivation of their liberty. The purpose or comfort of a deprivation of liberty is irrelevant. A parent can *potentially* consent to a deprivation if the child is under 16, in certain circumstances. A parent cannot consent if the young person is 16 or over. A corporate parent can never consent, regardless of age or whether there is an interim or final care order. In practice, the area in which you are most likely to experience issues in every day practice is around whether the level of deprivation requires a DOLs. The greater the level of supervision and control and the older the child, the more likely it is that court authorisation will be necessary. If all three elements of the test are deemed to be met, then an application for a DOLs order will need to be made to regularise those deprivations.

CHAPTER TWO

DEPRIVATION OF LIBERTY ORDERS FOR UNDER 18-YEAR-OLDS

In this chapter we will look at:

1. **The impact of a child's age**
2. **'Types' of cases**

Age of the child

This book considers Deprivation of Liberty ('DOLs') orders in relation to those who are classed as children, namely under the age of 18 years old. It is however important to note that children under 18 years are also looked at in differing ways depending on their actual age. This is the same in all areas of family for example how much weight will be given to a child's wishes and feelings in a private law dispute will often depend on their age.

In some circumstances there is a hard and fast rule about the age and the implication legally and in some circumstances it is more discretionary.

When considering making a DOLs application, the specific age of the child does have both a legal implication and also a bearing on the weight of their wishes in respect of any application therefore it is important to understand what the child's age does mean before making any application and is therefore the first step in this guide.

What implications can it have?

The answer to this question is 'many' namely:

1. What jurisdiction?
2. Can the child consent to the deprivations?
3. What restrictions will be classed as a deprivation?
4. The weight of the child's wishes and feelings

The first implication the age of the child will have is on what jurisdiction you are applying under (see chapter six):

1. If the child is under 16 years old then the application will have to be made under the court's Inherent Jurisdiction by way of the Senior Courts Act 1981;
2. If the child is aged 16 or 17 then the court *can* use the Inherent Jurisdiction but in the right circumstances can also use the jurisdiction of the Court of Protection

The next implication for DOLs applications is the ability or otherwise to consent to the deprivations sought. The younger the child the less like they will be considered to be competent to consent to the deprivations (see chapter one).

The age of the child can have significant bearing on what type of restrictions you will need and whether those restrictions class as a deprivation that requires a DOLs order or whether the restrictions can be implemented as reasonable use of parental responsibility held either by a parent or by a local authority by virtue of an interim care order, care order or under s20 CA 1989 (see chapter three).

Finally, the age of a child can have a bearing on the weight given to any wishes and feelings the child may have. This may not, in the end, have an impact on the need or otherwise for a DOLs order as this is subject to statutory considerations but it may impact on the need for the court to hear the voice of the child (and how that voice is heard eg through the children's guardian, sperate representation, and/or meeting the judge) or on the child's views about where they are placed for example.

Young children (aged 10 or under)

In summary:

1. Application has to be made under the Inherent Jurisdiction
2. Rare to have a DOLs application as it is likely that most restrictions would be considered a reasonable use of parental responsibility
3. Unlikely to be able to consent/ be *Gillick* competent
4. Limited weight given to their wishes and feelings
5. Voice of the child heard through their children's guardian and possibly a letter to the judge

Pre-teens (10-13 years old)

In summary:

1. Application has to be made under the Inherent Jurisdiction

2. Some of the main restrictions may be considered to require an application for a DOLs (eg level of supervision) but some will still be considered reasonable use of parental responsibility

3. Can consent themselves although this would be unusual (see chapter one for further information)

4. More weight is likely to be given to a child of this age's wishes and feelings

5. Voice of the child heard through their children's guardian but also likely through a letter to the judge and maybe a meeting with the judge

Teenagers (14-15 years old)

In summary:

1. Application has to be made under the Inherent Jurisdiction

2. More of the restrictions will be considered to require a DOLs order. For example, never being allowed to leave the placement unsupervised may not be considered to be a reasonable exercise of parental responsibility at that age

3. A child of this age is more likely to be assessed as having the ability to consent to the restrictions (again see chapter one for further information)

4. Substantial weight will be given to a child's wishes and feelings

5. Voice of the child to be heard through the children's guardian although consideration should be given to meeting with the Judge. The child's solicitor will also be expected to give due

consideration to the need for separate representation of a child where their views do not coincide with the children's guardian.

Young people (16 and over)

In summary:

1. Application can be made under the Inherent Jurisdiction but in circumstances where the child lacks capacity and is likely to need to be deprived of their liberty past the age of 18, it can also be made under the Court of Protection

2. Most if not all restrictions will be considered to require a DOLs order

3. A child of this age (where there are no additional needs) is considered to be competent and have the ability to consent to any restrictions (albeit this does not mean the court will accept that consent). If in the COP then the young person will have been determined to lack capacity to consent

4. The wishes and feelings of a child of this age are likely to be considered as almost determinative save for where a decision is being made in their best interest, contrary to their views or where they lack capacity

5. All attempts should be made for the voice of a child of this age to be heard by the court. In the family court, where views are aligned with the children's guardian this can be done through the children's guardian and can be supplemented by a letter or meeting with the judge. Where there is a difference of view then the child's solicitor should assess if the young person requires separation from the children's guardian and separate

representation. In the COP this will be done though a Rule 1.2 representative and/or a litigation friend

'Types' of cases

There are a number of 'types' of cases that might attract consideration of a DOLs application and it is important to consider what type of case you have before making any application.

There are 3 main categories of cases where a DOLs may be required:

1. Category 1- those that require their liberty to be deprived to protect them from lifestyle choices including gangs (eg county lines), exploitation, being beyond parental control due to matters such as absconding. It is important to remember that in these cases where there is no issue of capacity once a young person turns 18 the court will have no ability to make any orders in relation to their care

2. Category 2- those that have a mental health issue/learning difficulty/ diagnosis of a kind that impacts on their ability to function – common examples are ASD, ADHD, learning difficulties/disabilities etc

3. Category 3- those that are in a medical environment due to a mental health issue that requires medical attention/treatment for example those suffering from anorexia and subject to force feeding, serious self-harm etc

The test for a DOLs application and whether an order will be made remains the same for every category (chapter one) but when the category is considered alongside the age of the child (see above), this may impact on the following:

1. What jurisdiction you apply under – if it is a young person (16 or 17) then cases under category 2 (and some category 3) may best be applied for in the COP

2. What steps you may need to take before you issue an application:

    a. Category 1 – consideration should be given to whether a Secure Accommodation Order is the best order to be made in these circumstances

    b. Category 2 – if issuing in the COP a capacity assessment will need to be undertaken first

    c. Category 3 – consideration should be given as to who should make this application (local authority or the hospital for example), whether a capacity assessment should be undertaken if thought is being given to an application in the COP

    d. Further information on determining whether to issue in the COP or family court can be found in Chapter 5.

Summary

It is very important to consider both the age of the child and the 'category' of case at the start of any consideration of an application for a DOLs order as it will influence a number of the initial decisions for the making of any DOLs application.

CHAPTER THREE

WHEN DOLS AUTHORISATIONS ARE NOT NECESSARY OR APPROPRIATE

This chapter sets out:

1. Restrictions that do not require court authorisation through a DOLs regime:

    a. Exercise of parental responsibility- use of technology and contact

2. Restrictions that cannot be authorised through a DOLs regime

    a. Welfare

    b. Education

3. Secure accommodation orders vs DOLs

Restrictions that do not require court authorisation through a DOLs regime

There have been several cases in which the court has commented on the "creep" in DOLs applications to the courts. In essence, local authorities, likely out of an abundance of caution, are making applications for DOLs orders to authorise "restrictions" which are better characterised as the management of aspects of care or the lawful exercise of corporate responsibility and may better be described as interferences (albeit necessary and proportionate) with Article 8 rights rather than a fundamental breach of the child or young person's Article 5 rights. It is important to consider this when thinking about whether or not you need to make an application.

Use of technology and contact with families

At one stage many local authorities felt obliged to apply to the court for authorisation to restrict a child or young person's access to the internet, social media and phones ("use of technology"), as well as contact with family members, in circumstances where there was also a DOLs regime in place.

The legal framework for such restrictions was considered by MacDonald J in *Manchester City Council v P (Refusal of Restrictions on Mobile Phone) (*Rev1) [2023] EWHC 133 (Fam*)*. MacDonald J acknowledged that to date the court's approach (including his own) had been that such restrictions would require a DOLs order. However, upon reflection, the removal of a phone and limitation on internet use do not, in most cases, constitute a deprivation of P's physical liberty. Restrictions on P's phone use were not required to ensure the effectiveness of the current DOLs in place to stop her from leaving the placement, nor would the current DOLs be rendered ineffective without restrictions on phone use. Just because a restriction on phone use forms part of the overall regime in place at the placement, it does not follow that the restrictions need to be authorised under the auspices of a DOLs order. MacDonald J concluded:

> "*The difference between deprivation of and restriction upon liberty is one of degree or intensity and not one of nature or substance. But there is nonetheless a difference and that difference can have*

consequences. As I have noted above, restrictions of the type being imposed on P with respect to the use of her mobile phone, tablet and laptop, and concomitant limitations on her access to social media, are most naturally characterised as an interference with her Art 8 right to respect for private and family life." [50]

Restrictions in the use of technology are more properly described as an interference with the Article 8 right to private and family life, rather than Article 5.

The court confirmed that the appropriate way for a local authority to restrict and regulate the use of technology, in most cases, is through the exercise of its parental responsibility under s33(3)(b) Children Act 1989 [44]. Where the use of a phone or tablet is a source of significant harm for a child, then it is a proper exercise of parental responsibility for a parent to confiscate the item and/or restrict its use. Such restrictions could include not paying the phone bill or providing top ups or limiting Wi-Fi access. It is not a decision of such magnitude that it must go before the court. However, if physical restraint or force is required to remove a phone from a child, even if the steps are being taken to prevent significant harm to that child or young person, then those steps would require the court's approval [60].

This is not to say that the court cannot ever authorise DOLs in respect of technology use or contact, but as a general rule a local authority does not need to apply to the court to do so. The court anticipates that applications for DOLs orders in respect of technology use will only be necessary in a small number of cases. A circumstance in which it is envisaged that a DOLs order may be necessary could be to regulate phone use for a 17-year-old when a local authority does not share parental responsibility.

Contact

Where a local authority holds a care order for a child it is also entitled to restrict contact between the child and its parents as an exercise of its parental responsibility and therefore does not require an application to the court (although a suspension of contact would require an application under s34(4) Children Act 1989).

Restrictions that cannot be authorised through a DOLs

As well as there being some restrictions that should not be made by way of a DOLs order there are some restrictions that *cannot* be made by way of a DOLs order and it is important that when considering making an application for a DOLs order you are aware of the limitations.

Welfare

One limitation is welfare only decisions. In *A Local Authority v LB (acting by her Guardian) and others [2025] EWHC 1264 (Fam),* Mr David Lock KC, sitting as a Deputy High Court Judge, was invited to authorise a deprivation of liberty for "welfare" reasons. The court emphasised that just because a local authority has parental responsibility by virtue of a care order in is favour, this does not mean it is entitled to authorise a placement to impose restrictions amounting to a deprivation a liberty. In this case, A Local Authority accepted that it sought restrictions to prevent the child from absconding to live with the mother. A Local Authority accepted, and the court agreed, that depriving a child of its liberty for pure welfare reasons or to prevent absconding did not fall within article 5(1).

Education

Another is to ensure education. In the same case A Local Authority then sought alternatively to persuade the court that a deprivation was necessary under article 5(1)(d), namely "for the purpose of educational supervision". Mr David Lock KC accepted that whilst educational supervision encompasses a wide concept, going far beyond a classroom-based education but "*..it cannot be wholly equated with a child's welfare and restrictions and a deprivation of liberty cannot be justified under this part of the convention primarily to prevent a child absconding*" [25].

A local authority can seek authorisation for restrictions amounting to deprivations of a child's liberty in order to deliver educational support, and such restrictions can be both necessary and proportionate, but evidence of the same must be before the court. In this particular case, the child was receiving some assistance with life skills at the placement, but this fell far short of the evidence required to satisfy that it fell under article 5(1)(d).

Section 25 secure accommodation orders

It is often the case that a secure accommodation placement under section 25 Children Act 1989 would be the preferred placement for children or young people who require restrictions on their liberty under the category of "life choices".

However, due to the significant dearth of secure accommodation, local authorities are increasingly having to look to alternative placement options and these are often underpinned by a DOLs order. Consideration of the statutory framework for secure accommodation orders falls outside the scope of this guide but if a child or young person is accommodated in a secure placement under s25 Children

Act 1989 then a DOLs order will not be required; the necessary restrictions are authorised under s25 Children Act 1989.

Local authorities generally will be expected to have considered the appropriateness/ availability of secure accommodation prior to making an application for a DOLs order and may be expected to address the court on why a secure accommodation order is not being sought (see chapter four for further information on what information the local authority will need to provide in this regard)

Summary

Not all restrictions require a DOLs; restrictions on technology use and contact can be regulated by a local authority under its exercise of parental responsibility. There are also some kinds of restrictions that cannot be regulated by a DOL; education and welfare reasons cannot be used to justify a DOL order.

CHAPTER FOUR

PROCEDURE UNDER THE INHERENT JURISDICTION

This chapter sets out:

1. **S100 Children Act 1989 – Circumstances in which leave will be granted**
2. **The application**
3. **Parties**
4. **Court allocation**
5. **The first hearing**
6. **Subsequent hearings**
7. **The final order**
8. **Variation and renewal**

S100 Children Act 1989

A local authority must apply for the court's leave to make an application for any DOLs order under the inherent jurisdiction. S100 of the Children Act 1989 sets out the circumstances in which such leave will be granted (see appendix).

As orders under the inherent jurisdiction are orders of last resort, a local authority must be able to satisfy the court that an alternative order cannot achieve the same means. In the case of a DOLs order, the court may need to be satisfied that a secure accommodation order (under s25 CA 1989) cannot or should not be made. This was confirmed by Mr David Locke KC sitting as a Deputy Judge of the High Court in *A Local Authority v LB (acting by her Guardian) and others* [2025] EWHC 1264 (Fam)

> *12. I consider that, consistent with the approach taken by the Supreme Court in Re T, s25 accommodation and DOLS orders should not be seen as alternatives to be used by local authorities at their option. Where a child could be accommodated in secure accommodation under the s25 route, that option should be used where available. Use of the inherent jurisdiction should thus be limited to cases where a local authority provides clear evidence to explain why the s25 statutory framework, with its protections for the child, has not been used.*

Therefore, the social work evidence should make clear the steps that have been taken to identify section 25 accommodation.

The application

The application must be made on form C66. The application must state, with reasons, whether the application needs to be heard within a) 4 hours, b) 24 hours, c) 3 days, or d) 5 days. The local authority should be ready for the case to be heard within the timescale requested! This includes ensuring the availability of counsel and an electronic bundle.

The local authority will need to provide the following documents with the application:

i. Child's birth certificate

ii. Care Order (if appropriate)

iii. Social work statement

iv. Care Plan

The local authority social work statement should provide the following information:

i. the child's background;

ii. whether there are related care proceedings – ongoing, to be issued or completed;

iii. details of the proposed placement including background to both provider and property, staffing, training and whether regulated or unregulated;

iv. education plan;

v. CAMHS or other NHS involvement and services;

vi. proposed contact arrangements

vii. the views of the child, their parents, and the IRO (where known)

In relation to the detail of the DOLs sought, the social work statement will need to specifically identify the restrictions and the length of time for which it is anticipated that the restrictions will be required. The local authority must also make it clear why the restrictions are necessary and proportionate and no lesser regime can meet the child's welfare needs.

The Parties

The local authority will most likely be the applicant to the proceedings. Parents with parental responsibility are automatically parties (although if the DOLs is a freestanding application and there are no parallel care proceedings, they will not have automatic legal aid and so are often litigants in person).

Proceedings under the inherent jurisdiction are not "specified proceedings" for the purposes of an appointment of a guardian pursuant to s41 of the Children Act 1989. As such, the appointment of a guardian is not automatic and the court will need to appoint one. If the hearing has been listed on extremely short notice, the appointment may not have taken place in time for the hearing, but should have done by the time of a review hearing. If there are parallel or previous care proceedings, this will ideally be the same guardian.

National DOLs list

On 11th October 2023, the Revised National Listing Protocol for applications that seek Deprivation of Liberty Orders relating to children under the inherent jurisdiction was issued.

In summary, all initial applications for a DOLs shall be dealt with as part of the National DOL list (previously National DOL Court). C66 applications should be issued centrally in the Royal Courts of Justice (RCJ) to rcj.nationaldolslist@justice.gov.uk.

In practice, if there are concurrent care proceedings, and the parties and the court are expecting an imminent application for a DOLs, then the case may go before the allocated judge for the proceedings.

The revised protocol for the national DOLs list requests that, where possible, urgent applications should not be issued on a Friday as this will be particularly difficult for the listing team at the RCJ. Unless the application is one of exceptional urgency, first applications should preferably be made between Monday and Thursday.

First hearing

Generally the first hearing will be before either a Judge of the Family Division or a s9 Deputy Judge of the High Court hearing the national DOLs list, unless the local authority requests a transfer out to the local family court for the first hearing and can confirm that a s9 judge is available and willing to deal with the hearing as required (in practice, this is likely to be when there are parallel care proceedings allocated to a s9 judge who has confirmed they could accommodate the DOLs hearing).

The first hearing of the application in the national DOLs list will take place remotely. It is likely to be brief and the court will make a decision as to whether the local authority has provided the requisite evidence to satisfy it that the DOLs order should be made. The court will make the order for the shortest time necessary and list a review hearing which may be transferred back to the local family court.

The draft order from the first hearing should address:

1. permission to the local authority to make the application
2. the scope of the DOL restrictions
3. the name/identity of the placement;
4. any specific requirements or pre-conditions (e.g. one female member of staff to be on site at all times);
5. notification to Ofsted if placement is unregulated;

6. contact;

7. education;

8. appointment of a Guardian;

9. review / next hearing and before whom? (i.e. where possible the s.9 judge to whom the case has been/will be allocated in the local court should be identified in the first directions order).

Subsequent hearings

It is unusual for DOLs proceedings to be particularly protracted. In circumstances where all parties agree with the terms and duration of a DOLs then the proceedings may be capable of resolution with a limited number of hearings. although the court may direct the guardian to file and serve an analysis before proceedings conclude. Any dispute as to specific terms or length of the DOLs can usually be resolved on submissions without oral evidence.

It may be that the child themselves challenges the making of the DOLs, or objects to specific terms or the length of the same. If the child's solicitor does not consider that the child has litigation capacity, then these views shall be expressed to the court as their wishes and feelings. If, however, the child's solicitor deems that the child does have litigation capacity, there will need to be consideration of the child's separate representation and necessary directions made for this, with the opportunity for the child's position to be properly advocated at a hearing, either on submissions or with cross examination of the social worker and/or guardian.

The final order

A DOLs order can be made for a maximum period of 12 months although whether this is an appropriate length will depend on the individual circumstances of each case.

The restrictions authorised are permissive, that is they do not need to be implemented at all times but rather this means that the placement has permission to use them as and when they are required.

Variation and renewal

A local authority will need to make further applications if either a) the current restrictions need varying or b) the current restrictions need extending beyond the current term. In each case, the appropriate evidence to support the orders sought will need to be provided. A change in a child's placement will require an immediate application for variation of a DOLs, regardless of whether the type of restrictions proposed to be in place at the new placement will be the same.

Applications for renewals and extensions should also be made in good time and the court will not look favourably upon local authorities making last minute applications when the need for the application has been known for some time.

Summary

A local authority needs the court's leave to apply for a DOLs and it will need to provide a number of documents with its application, including a social work statement addressing relevant factors. Generally, the first hearing in the application will be heard remotely by the national DOL list with directions then made for the future progression of the case. Applications for variation and/or renewal should be made in a timely fashion.

CHAPTER FIVE

PLACEMENTS FOR CHILDREN SUBJECT TO A DOLS

This chapter considers:

- **The Court's function in relation to establishing whether a placement is registered or unregistered for a child placed there under a DOLs**

The Court's function in relation to establishing whether a placement is registered or unregistered for a child placed there under a DOLs

In September 2023, the President of the Family Division issued its Revised Guidance on the court's approach to unregistered placements.

In 2019, Guidance had been issued setting out the steps that courts should take in order to establish whether a placement in which a child was placed under a DOLs was registered, and if not, the steps to be taken towards registration. However, this placed considerable burdens on the court and was not a proper part of the court's function. Therefore, the Revised Guidance replaces the 2019 Guidance and instead sets out that:

> [5] *It is not for the Court to become a regulatory body or the overseer of the regulatory process. The Court's role in deprivation of liberty applications, is to exercise its inherent jurisdiction to ensure that any deprivation of liberty is not itself unlawful, whether as an unlawful*

> *detention under the common law, or a breach of Article 5 of the ECHR. That is the extent of the Court's powers, and the Court's role should not go beyond those powers.*

The President has confirmed that he considers that it is appropriate for the court to enquire as to whether the placement proposed is registered or unregistered. If the placement is unregistered, then the court "should enquire as to why the local authority considers an unregistered placement is in the best interests of the child" [para 8 of the Guidance] and may order the local authority to inform Ofsted/CIW within seven days of placing a child in an unregistered placement.

The Court of Appeal in *A Mother v Derby City Council [2021] EWCA Civ 1867* held that the inherent jurisdiction may be used to authorise a deprivation of liberty for a child under the age of 16 in an unregistered children's home, so long as the requirements set out by the Supreme Court in *Re T* are met. In *A Mother,* Sir Andrew MacFarlane provides detailed discussion in respect of the statutory schemes for the placement of children who are looked after by local authorities and the lawfulness of the placement of a child in an unregistered children's home. His conclusion was that

> "*The judgments in Re T endorse the exercise of the inherent jurisdiction to authorise deprivation of liberty with respect to a placement in an unregistered children's home, where imperative conditions of necessity justify doing so and there is no alternative available.*" [83]

> *"We have found that the scheme does not allow unregistered placements, but does not expressly prohibit them. In those circumstances, as in Re T, where conditions of imperative necessity require, the common law steps in and allows the High Court to exercise its inherent jurisdiction. That exercise of the inherent*

jurisdiction is not in breach of Art 5 and nor does it cut across the statutory scheme. As it is not the High Court that is making the placement, the exercise of the inherent jurisdiction is not part of the statutory scheme at all. In this respect, the situation is exactly as it was in Re T where the Supreme Court did not feel the need to read any words into the statute." [88]

Therefore, the court does have jurisdiction, in the appropriate case, to authorise the DOLs for a child placed in an unregistered placement. The President notes that in withdrawing the 2019 Guidance, this is not ignoring the benefits of a placement in in a registered placement over an unregistered placement, but is instead an acknowledgement that the court "should restrict its considerations and orders to its own functions" [7].

Summary

DOLs can be authorised for a child in an unregistered placement so long as a local authority can explain to the court why such placement is in the child's best interests.

CHAPTER SIX

WHERE TO ISSUE – FAMILY COURT OR COURT OF PROTECTION?

This chapter sets out:

1. **Factors in determining whether an application should be made in the family court or the Court of Protection:**

    a. **Under 16 vs 16 and 17-year-olds**

    b. **Relevant factors for 16 and 17-year-olds**

2. **Transfer between the family court and the Court of Protection**

Once you are satisfied that an application for DOLs is required, then the next consideration will be whether to issue under the inherent jurisdiction of the family court, or in the Court of Protection.

Under 16 vs 16 and 17-year-olds

Age

As discussed previously (in chapter two) the age of the child or young person is the first relevant matter to consider:

- If a child is under 16, the application must be issued in the Family Court under the Inherent Jurisdiction

- If the young person is aged 16 or 17, you have a choice as to whether to issue in the Family Court or the Court of Protection

For a more detailed consideration of the impact of age on DOLs order applications see chapter two.

Relevant matters when determining where to issue for 16 and 17-year-olds

There are a number of considerations which will affect the appropriate jurisdiction for the issuing of the application. They include the likely need for orders post-18 i.e. where the young person has life-long difficulties which will likely require ongoing deprivations, the urgency of the application, and whether there are existing care proceedings. Considering the following questions should provide you with assistance in determining where best to issue:

- Is this a young person beyond parental control where the need for the DOLs does not relate to mental health or learning difficulties? If so, the DOLs could not continue post-18 and so the application should be made in the family court

- Is there likely to be a need for long term restrictions after the young person turns 18 due to mental health difficulties or learning difficulties? If so, the DOLs are likely to be required post-18 and so the application should be made in the Court of Protection

- Is the young person in a medical setting and requiring authorisations relating to their medical care? If so, the application is probably best made in the Court of Protection, but such applications are normally made- and best made- by the NHS trust treating the child or young person, rather than the local authority.

- Are there current care proceedings? If so, and the need for the DOLs is urgent, then it may be quicker to make the application under the inherent jurisdiction within those care proceedings.

- Are there outstanding issues relating to care planning which are likely to be resolved before the child's 18th birthday? If so, then the family court is likely to be appropriate.

Transfer between the Family Court and the Court of Protection

If you find you have issued under one jurisdiction but the development of the case better lends itself to another jurisdiction then there are clear guidelines for how to transfer from one jurisdiction to another.

Article 2 of the Mental Capacity Act sets out the considerations and the process for the transfer of cases from the Court of Protection to the Family Court.

Transfers from the Court of Protection to a court having jurisdiction under the Children Act

(1) This article applies to any proceedings in the Court of Protection which relate to a person under 18.

(2) The Court of Protection may direct the transfer of the whole or part of the proceedings to a court having jurisdiction under the Children Act where it considers that in all the circumstances, it is just and convenient to transfer the proceedings.

(3) In making a determination, the Court of Protection must have regard to—

(a) whether the proceedings should be heard together with other proceedings that are pending in a court having jurisdiction under the Children Act;

(b) whether any order that may be made by a court having jurisdiction under that Act is likely to be a more appropriate way of dealing with the proceedings;

(c) the need to meet any requirements that would apply if the proceedings had been started in a court having jurisdiction under the Children Act; and

(d) any other matter that the court considers relevant.

(4) The Court of Protection—

(a) may exercise the power to make an order under paragraph (2) on an application or on its own initiative; and

(b) where it orders a transfer, must give reasons for its decision.

(5) Any proceedings transferred under this article—

(a) are to be treated for all purposes as if they were proceedings under the Children Act which had been started in a court having jurisdiction under that Act; and

(b) are to be dealt with after the transfer in accordance with directions given by a court having jurisdiction under that Act.

In reverse, Article 3 sets out the process for the transfer of cases from the Family Court to the Court of Protection.

Transfers from a court having jurisdiction under the Children Act to the Court of Protection

(1) This article applies to any proceedings in a court having jurisdiction under the Children Act which relate to a person under 18.

(2) A court having jurisdiction under the Children Act may direct the transfer of the whole or part of the proceedings to the Court of Protection where it considers that in all circumstances, it is just and convenient to transfer the proceedings.

(3) In making a determination, the court having jurisdiction under the Children Act must have regard to—

(a) whether the proceedings should be heard together with other proceedings that are pending in the Court of Protection;

(b) whether any order that may be made by the Court of Protection is likely to be a more appropriate way of dealing with the proceedings;

(c) the extent to which any order made as respects a person who lacks capacity is likely to continue to have effect when that person reaches 18; and

(d) any other matter that the court considers relevant.

(4) A court having jurisdiction under the Children Act—

(a) may exercise the power to make an order under paragraph (2) on an application or on its own initiative; and

(b) where it orders a transfer, must give reasons for its decision.

(5) Any proceedings transferred under this article—

(a) are to be treated for all purposes as if they were proceedings under the Mental Capacity Act 2005 which had been started in the Court of Protection; and

(b) are to be dealt with after the transfer in accordance with directions given by the Court of Protection.

In *B (A Local Authority) v RM & Ors [2010] EWHC B31* Hadley J (as he then was) considers circumstances in which a case may be transferred under Article 3 from the Court of Protection to the Family Court

> *[28] That raises the question particularly under Article 3(3)(d) as to what matters the Court should take into account in deciding whether to exercise these powers and to adopt this approach. An ex tempore judgment in a case on its own facts is no basis for attempting an exhaustive analysis of these issues; nevertheless, a number of matters suggest themselves, matters which may often be relevant in the relatively small number of cases in which this issue is likely to arise. One, is the child over 16? Otherwise of course, there is no power. Two, does the child manifestly lack capacity in respect of the principal decisions which are to be made in the Children Act proceedings? Three, are the disabilities which give rise to lack of capacity lifelong or at least long-term? Four, can the decisions which arise in respect of the child's welfare all be taken and all issues resolved during the child's minority? Five, does the Court of*

Protection have powers or procedures more appropriate to the resolution of outstanding issues than are available under the Children Act? Six, can the child's welfare needs be fully met by the exercise of Court of Protection powers? These provisional thoughts are intended to put some flesh on to the provisions of Article 3(3); no doubt, other issues will arise in other cases. The essential thrust, however, is whether looking at the individual needs of the specific young person, it can be said that their welfare will be better safeguarded within the Court of Protection than it would be under the Children Act.

The President of the Family Division issued guidance ('Practice Guidance in respect of Transition of Matters from the National DOL List to the Court of Protection') in January 2025. The directions that should be sought from the National DOL court are:

1. That the applicant, within a specified timeframe, issues the relevant COP1 application to the appropriate regional hub court for consideration by a judge of Tier 2 level

2. The papers from the proceedings thus far are released into the COP proceedings.

In *Re A-F No. 2* [2018] EWHC 2129 Sir James Munby endorsed the approach taken in *B (A Local Authority)* and further considered the relevant factors in determining whether proceedings should be transferred from the Family Court to the Court of Protection, noting that in *B (A Local Authority),* there was an application for a care order but no care order in place. In *Re A-F* the subject children were already subject to care orders and Sir James Munby concluded that their cases should remain in the Family Court for the following reasons [12]:

(i) There can be no sensible basis for discharging any of the care orders which are already in place. The children require the continuing protection of such aspects of the care regime as LAC reviews and the support of an IRO.

(ii) While the care orders remain in place, the Family Court has a continuing, if much reduced, potential role in the lives of the children – for instance, if issues in relation to contact require to be determined in accordance with section 34 of the 1989 Act.

(iii) For the time being, at least until they are approaching their eighteenth birthdays, the children are the responsibility of the local authority's Children's Social Care (LAC) Teams, who are, in the nature of things, much more familiar with practice and procedure in the Family Court and the Family Division than with practice and procedure in the Court of Protection.

(iv) The children's guardians will be able to continue exercising that role so long as the cases remain within the Family Court and the Family Division; it is, at the least, doubtful whether they would be able to act as litigation friends in the Court of Protection

(v) It *may* be easier to ensure judicial continuity if there is no transfer.

(vi) Put shortly, the benefits weigh heavily in favour of maintaining the forensic status quo. There are, in contrast, so far as I can see, no reasons for thinking that, to adopt Hedley J's words, the children's welfare will be better safeguarded within the Court of Protection.

Where proceedings are transferred from the Family Court to the Court of Protection, any involvement of Cafcass will come to an end, in accordance with the Practice Note of the Official Solicitor to the

Senior Courts: Appointment in Family Proceedings and Proceedings under the Inherent Jurisdiction relating to Adults, January 2017.

As a reminder, the relevant test and appropriate considerations for DOLs orders are the same regardless of whether the application is issued in the family court or COP (or transferred from one to the other).

Parallel family and COP proceedings

If there are existing care proceedings and it is also anticipated that longer term restrictions will be required once the child turns 18, then inherent jurisdiction and COP proceedings can run alongside one another. If a DOLs application was made urgently within the care proceedings, it may be appropriate for the DOLs proceedings then to be transferred from the family court to COP. The case can be allocated to a judge who sits in both the family court and COP to enable this to happen. This will ensure that there is a smooth transition once the child turns 18.

Summary

The age of the child or young person is the key determining factor in where to issue. For, under 16sthe application must be issued in the family court. For 16–17-year-olds, the application can be issued in either the family court or COP and there are a number of relevant considerations to help you decide which is the most appropriate. It is possible for cases to transfer from the family court to COP and vice versa, and again there are a number of considerations when deciding if this may be appropriate.

CHAPTER SEVEN

INTRODUCTION TO THE COURT OF PROTECTION

In this chapter we will discuss:

1. **Introduction to the Court of Protection (COP)**

2. **Mental capacity including assessment of the same**

3. **Parties including litigation friends**

Introduction to the COP

The Court of Protection oversees the operation of the Mental Capacity Act 2005 ('MCA') and deals with all issues, including financial and serious healthcare matters, concerning people who lack the mental capacity to make their own decisions.

The court also tries to resolve all disputes when the person's carer, healthcare worker or social worker disagree about what is in the person's best interests, or when the views conflict in relation to property and welfare.

The court hears important cases, such as whether the NHS should withdraw treatment, whether a serious medical treatment decision is in a person's best interests, or whether it is in a person's best interests to be deprived of their liberty.

Cases can be brought to the court by family members, as well as advocates and professionals involved in decisions.

This guide's focus is on the practical steps required when the COP is called upon to deprive a young person (namely a child of 16 or 17) of their liberty. It is important to note therefore that the Deprivation of Liberty Safeguards (or DOLS with a capital 'S') process is not discussed in this guide in any detail as this would only apply to adults over 18 years old.

Mental Capacity

When to consider mental capacity

Having considered the points set out in chapter six of this book you should have a good idea whether the COP is an option for your case. The questions to ask yourself are:

1. Is the child a young person ie are they 16 or 17 years old?
2. Do they lack capacity?
3. Is any potential DOLs likely to need to last into adulthood? Ie is it a condition that is going to persist past the age of 18?

If the answer to all three of these is 'yes', then you should consider whether your application is best made in the COP rather than under the Inherent Jurisdiction.

What is mental capacity?

The COP is governed by the Mental Capacity Act 2005 (MCA) and in order to make an application to the COP the young person would need to be assessed as lacking mental capacity as defined in the MCA (the full sections of the statute are replicated in the appendix of this guide).

Section 1 of the MCA sets out the five key principles which emphasise its fundamental concepts and core values. In summary these are:

1. Every adult has the right to make his or her own decisions and must be assumed to have capacity to do so unless it is proved otherwise.

2. People must be supported as much as possible to make their own decisions before anyone concludes that they cannot do so.

3. People have the right to make what others might regard as unwise or eccentric decisions. Everyone has their own values, beliefs and preferences which may not be the same as those of other people. People cannot be treated as lacking capacity for that reason.

4. Anything done for, or on behalf of, a person who lacks mental capacity must be done in their best interests.

5. Anything done for, or on behalf of, people without capacity should be the least restrictive of their basic rights and freedoms.

It should also be noted that issues of capacity are decision specific, so for the purposes of this guide the decisions being looked at are does the young person have the capacity to decide what placement they should reside in and whether or not they should be subject to a DOLs order.

Assessment of capacity

An assessment of a young person's capacity can be undertaken by a suitably qualified social worker or a psychologist or psychiatrist. In the case of a psychologist or psychiatrist this can be a treating clinician (particular at the start of proceedings) or a joint expert instructed during the course of proceedings.

In order to assess capacity the MCA sets out the two-stage test in section 2 of the act which in summary is:

1. Does the person have an impairment of their mind or brain, whether as a result of an illness, or external factors such as alcohol or drug use?

2. Does the impairment mean the person is unable to make a specific decision when they need to?

When assessing capacity the assessor is asked to look at whether the person can:

1. Understand the information relating to the decision

2. Weigh up that information

3. Remember that information for long enough to make their decision

4. Communicate their decision (whether verbally, using sign language, or by other means)

It is also important to bear in mind that a person's capacity can fluctuate and must be kept under review. This is particularly pertinent when linked with the second of the five key principles set out above the principle that people should be supported to make decisions by themselves where possible, as providing support or work to try and help the young person gain capacity in these areas could lead to a need to reassess capacity at regular intervals.

Parties

Parties to proceedings that are not the young person

This can be a little confusing especially when a case has started under the Inherent Jurisdiction and is then moved to the COP as the parties then change.

Unless the court directs otherwise the parties to the proceedings are the applicant and any person named on the application form as a respondent and files an acknowledgment of service. The court is able to join other people as a party if it considers it 'desirable to do so for the purpose of dealing with the application'.

In the COP the applicant is most often the local authority but can also be other relevant bodies such as an NHS Trust on behalf of a hospital where the young person is receiving some form of treatment.

In relation to other parties in these types of cases the most likely people that will hold an interest are parents, adult siblings, and other types of carers (special guardianship, foster carers etc).

It is noted that in a lot of these cases the young person will have been removed from their family some time before this application under a final care order and may not have had any recent contact with, for example a parent they have been removed from for some time. Care should be taken around informing interested people in these circumstances. It is right that a DOLs order cannot be used to regularise or limit contact but be aware if there are already limits to contact in place especially if the young person has clearly expressed views.

It is also worth noting that, unlike in care proceedings in the family court, parents/carers/family members are not automatically entitled to legal aid and so in many cases they will be unrepresented.

If you as the applicant are satisfied that it is appropriate to have conversations with the relevant people it is important to discuss with them what role they would wish to play:

a. Do they wish to seek to be made a formal party and submit evidence or would they wish to be an interested party who is kept informed of the proceedings and provides their view to the applicant which will be given to the court but do not play a formal role in court

b. Would they wish to put themselves forward to act as a litigation friend for the young person in these proceedings

c. Would they wish to put themselves forward as the Rule 1.2 representative for the young person

These issues should be discussed prior to making an application and any issues discussed at the first hearing so that anyone that wishes to make representations in relation to party status can be invited to attend that hearing so that this can be considered without causing delay in proceedings.

The young person/ litigation friend

Under the Inherent Jurisdiction the young person would have a children's guardian appointed by the court. In the COP the young person will require a litigation friend.

In cases where they start in the Inherent Jurisdiction and move to the COP the children's guardian will not continue to be appointed. Therefore, consideration will then need to be given as to who can act as the Litigation Friend.

In the first instance consideration should be given as to whether any of the interested parties are suitable for example a parent or adult sibling. If it is a case where the young person requires a DOLs order following care proceedings it is often not appropriate for a parent to act as a Litigation Friend as they have already been determined by the court to not be able to effectively exercise their parental responsibility in the best interest of the child. There are however a number of cases where a parent or carer may be the appropriate person where for example the DOLs order is required due to longstanding mental health issues or disability and there is no question as to the parenting provided by the carer.

The court will want to see that all reasonable steps have been taken to explore these options for Litigation Friends. If there is no one else that can act as a Litigation Friend the COP will need to be asked to invite the Official Solicitor ('OS') to act as the Litigation Friend of last resort. In order to limit delay, if this is going to be required, the court should be informed at the earliest opportunity (preferably in the application form) so that the OS can be brought on as soon as possible.

Once this invitation is made to the OS the court will also make an order for a financial assessment of the young person so that the OS can consider how its costs will be met.

Summary

The COP can be used to deprive 16 or 17-year-olds of their liberty if they are assessed to lack capacity. There is clear guidance as to how to assess capacity and what principles apply set out in the MCA 2005. It is imperative that steps are taken at the beginning to consider capacity and also the parties and roles of interested people in the proceedings; in particular consideration should be given at the earliest opportunity as to who can act as a Litigation Friend for the young person.

CHAPTER EIGHT

WORKING TOGETHER: TRANSITIONING AND PLANNING

In this chapter we will discuss:

1. **Transitioning from children to adult services**
2. **Needs for transition:**
    a. **Placements**
    b. **Education**
    c. **Healthcare**
3. **Those leaving the court process**

Transitioning from children to adult services

The inevitable difficulty in cases which concern 16 and 17-year-olds on the ground is the interplay between children's and adult services. Most pertinently this is likely to be within the local authority but can also be hospital wards, treating teams, support in the community, and placements.

One thing the court consistently makes clear is it will not be impressed by arguments between departments in the same organisations or between children and adult teams especially when it comes to arguments over budget.

It is important that discussions are held at the earliest opportunity and a clear plan made for how to transition the young person from children services to adult services. The best way to approach this is to have co-working professionals for example social workers that can both bring the expertise of each team and in particular what services are available to the young person now under children and going forward under adults. The sooner this is done the more detailed the information that can be provided to the court and the shorter proceedings will inevitably be.

By way of examples:

1. Adult social workers may be used to do capacity assessments whereas children social workers may not be

2. Identifying support services such as education, mentoring, respite services, enrichment

3. Funding of placements and support services

4. Identifying appropriate placements

The first step when considering if there will need to be this type of transition work is to consider if you think there are grounds to consider the young person lacks capacity (within the meaning of the MCA 2005 – see chapter seven). If the answer is 'yes' then thought needs to be given about undertaking or obtaining a capacity assessment and this should be the starting point of working alongside each other.

The very real importance of constructive, timely and effective working between agencies and departments was emphasised recently by Henke

J in *Re N (a Child) (Deprivation of Liberty Orders) [2025] EWHC 1690 (Fam).*

Needs to transition

Placement

One key area of transition planning for those young people who will be moving from children's services to adult's services within the court process, is where the young person will be living. Although this book is focused on the making of DOLs orders it is worth noting (as it has been elsewhere in this book) that DOLs orders are placement specific and therefore it will be imperative that consideration is given to where the young person will be living.

It is important to note that a DOLs made in the COP (in the same way as it is in the Inherent Jurisdiction) does not itself place a young person in a placement or give powers in themselves for them to be accommodated there; it is that the DOLs has to be linked to a placement.

Given the age we are considering, this is likely to be a time when thought is given to the long-term plans for the young person. If you have made an application to the COP then that is because the depriving authority are of the view that these restrictions are likely to need to last past the age of 18. It is therefore very likely that the application will need to cover whether the placement is appropriate once they attain that age or whether there is going to need to be a change of placement because for example the placement only accommodates those under 18 years old. Early discussion between children and adult's services may identify suitable accommodation quicker and more easily due to the pooling of resource information.

Looking at the suitability of placements ties in with wider transition planning as it would be beneficial to identify a long-term placement (if possible) at an early stage to limit the need for further sets of proceedings.

Education

Education is also a key factor in transitioning from children to adult social care; especially where the young person has an Educational Health Care Plan (EHCP). Some cease at 18 but there are some plans that entitle the young person to post-18 education pursuant to the Children's and Families Act 2014. This will cover more formal education such as Maths and English but could also include learning life skills to create more independence. It is important that there is continuity of provision for education so that the young person does not suffer any detriment due to a break in this provision.

Healthcare

Healthcare needs may be stable or increasing as the young person gets older. It will be important to ensure that the right healthcare teams are involved and that any transition of healthcare team is done seamlessly so that there is no break in meeting the young person's health needs. It is also a time in their life where changes will have taken place to them physically (as teenagers) and this may require continuing assessments by departments such as occupational therapy and health.

Those leaving the court process

It may also be the case that a young person who is the subject of a DOLs order by virtue of the Inherent Jurisdiction (as they have capacity) may then not require or be eligible for continued intervention from the court once they turn 18. They are however likely to be eligible for some form of leaving care provisions and may need assistance with transitioning back into the community for example accommodation, financial support and any other support services such as substance misuse or job seeking. It is important that any progress that a young person has made whilst subject to the DOLs order is not undone at the end of it and this transition to adult services is equally important to address early.

Summary

Pre-planning is hugely important in these types of cases to avoid delay, costs and criticisms. It is advisable for children and adult teams to work together to come up with a comprehensive plan of the services and placement underpinning the DOLs order or for when the young person leaves the court system.

CHAPTER NINE

PROCEDURE FOR APPLICATIONS IN THE COURT OF PROTECTION

In this chapter we will discuss:

1. **How to apply for a DOLs order in the COP (Deprivation of Liberty Safeguards, Re X, general application)**

2. **Test to apply**

3. **Urgent applications**

How to apply

There are a variety of ways to make a DOLs order application in the COP namely:

1. By way of standard authorisation under schedule 1A MCA 2005 (Deprivation of Liberty Safeguards)

2. *Re X* procedure/ streamlined process

3. A general application to the COP

Schedule 1A MCA 2005 (Deprivation of Liberty Safeguards)

Whilst this may be an option when considering an application for a DOLs for a person over the age of 18 it is not an option for young people (16/17 years olds) due to the qualifying requirements that are set out in s12(1) that refer to an 'age requirement' which is further defined in s13:

> 'the relevant person meets the age requirement if he has reached 18'

This is therefore not an option in the cases we are considering.

Streamlined process / Re X procedure

The next option is the process under s16(2) MCA 2005 for an order authorising a deprivation of liberty under s4A(3) and (4). The relevant cases to refer to are:

1. *P (by his litigation friend the Official Solicitor) v Cheshire West and Chester Council and another; P and Q (by their litigation friend the Official Solicitor) v Surrey County* Council [2014] UKSC 19 (the leading case in respect of DOLs and discussed in chapter 2)

2. *Re X and Others (Deprivation of Liberty)* [2014] EWCOP 25

3. *Re X and Others (Deprivation of Liberty) (Number 2)* [2014] EWCOP 37.

Following the exponential increase in the need for a court to authorise a deprivation of liberty following *Cheshire West* the COP put in place a 'streamlined' process. The procedure for these applications is usually called the *Re X* procedure after the latter two cases in the above list. The procedure is set out at PD 11A and any application is made by way of a COPDOL11 form.

This procedure was designed to consider those applications which are not contentious and therefore there was a likely chance that the matter could be dealt with 'on the papers' without the need for any oral hearings. It is however clear that as well as dealing with streamlined applications it is also possible to use this procedure to determine non contentious applications involving 16 and 17-year-olds which the Safeguards do not allow.

The court will have to determine if it considers the case suitable for a streamlined process and the COPDOL11 form itself provides a number of trigger points that might indicate that this process is not suitable including:

1. Any contest by the young person or anyone else to any of the key parts of the form

2. Failure to consult with the young person and/or obtain any views from them or relevant people

3. Any objection raised by the young person

4. Any conflicts

5. Concerns about the information provided that could lead to the need for judicial scrutiny

6. Any other reason that the court considers an oral hearing is required

This form is substantial with a significant amount of information required to be input. It is worthwhile considering the questions in this form at an early stage so that thought can be given to what information needs to be collected in order to satisfy the court and limit delay; this is particularly important where a case will be moving between children services and adult services and there may need to be joint working in order to be able to obtain all the information to complete the form.

The court will want to want to have information about a number of matters including:

1. What the restrictions are and at what level

2. What work will be done with the young person to try and reduce the restrictions in the future (this of course may not be possible)

3. How long the order is sought for (an order can be made for a maximum of 12 months at any one time)

4. What training the staff members have in particular in relation to physical restraint

5. How the placement and staff enacting the DOLs order will be funded

6. Views of the young person and any relevant person

7. Evidence of their lack of capacity

8. Details of the care arrangements for the young person including care and/or support plan

It will be helpful to provide as much supporting evidence of each element as possible.

The court will also want to have information about:

1. The young person's eligibility for public funding (this can be complicated where for example there has been a significant inheritance or settlement)

2. Why it is thought this matter can proceed without an oral hearing

3. Confirmation that steps have been taken to notify the young person and the other relevant people

4. Whether a potential Rule 1.2 representative has been identified; this could be a friend or family member (see below) or another appropriate person such as an IMCA

The court will also want to know more about the family/ carers of the young person which should include:

1. Has there been a discussion with them about being a Rule 1.2 representative and do they wish to do this. If they do are they suitable to be a Rule 1.2 representative with reference to the young person's needs and the history of the young person's care. They do not have to agree with the application in order to be appointed as a Rule 1.2 representative

2. What the nature of the care that they have provided in the previous years has been for example are they carers who have looked after the young person with no issues and the time has come for a change in care plan or are they carers who have had involvement with the local authority due to neglectful care

3. What their views are on the application and if they disagree, what are their reasons

Once the application is issued the court will consider all of the pertinent information as set out above and ascertain if it can determine this application on the papers or whether an oral hearing will need to be listed. It should be noted an order cannot be made on the papers if there is no Rule 1.2 representative or litigation friend available to give a view on behalf of the young person.

Standard application

The majority of cases that involve 16/17-year-old young people are likely to require an oral hearing for one of the reasons set out above. Often it is due to this being the first time that accommodation and care planning will be considered by the COP alongside the DOLs order and therefore there will also need to be authorisation of placement and care and support plans not just the authorising of the deprivations.

This application would need to be made using a COP1 form which is the standard application form by which to instigate proceedings in the COP and will lead to the listing of an oral hearing.

Again, this is a comprehensive form that takes the applicant through the key pieces of information that will be required (much is the same as above). This application will need to be accompanied by a COP3 assessment of capacity (see chapter seven). If for any reason it is not possible to file a COP3 alongside the COP1 then a witness statement from the social worker must be filed explaining why this assessment has not been possible, the attempts made and on what basis the applicant believes that the young person lacks capacity (Practice Direction 9A, para 14).

A COP1B Annex B must also be filed which is a statement from the social worker in support of your application setting out why you require this order and including any other supporting information such as information from the proposed placement as to how the staff are trained to undertake restraint.

It will be important that the statement sets out:

1. What the restrictions are and at what level
2. What work will be done with the young person to try and reduce the restrictions in the future (this of course may not be possible)
3. How long the order is sought for (an order can be made for a maximum of 12 months at any one time)
4. What training the staff members have in particular in relation to physical restraint
5. How the placement and staff enacting the DOLs order will be funded
6. Views of the young person and any relevant person
7. Details of the care arrangements for the young person including care and/or support plan

Which procedure?

More recently which procedure to be used for young people has been considered by Her Honour Judge Hilder in *Bolton Council v KL* [2022] EWCOP 24. This case considered not only the approach of the court to applications in relation to young people but more specifically when the streamlined/ *Re X* procedure is appropriate to be used in relation to a young person.

The key learning from that case is that:

1. HHJ Hilder was clear that the streamlined/*Re X* procedure, whilst allowing for applications to be made in relation to young people was not designed with those cases in mind

2. She emphasised the point of transition that young people are at from children's to adult services and the potential pitfalls and difficulties that this transition can cause and that may require more hands on judicial oversight

3. More than any other age group the use of restraint is said to be necessary and in the person's 'best interest' which again might require more hands on judicial oversight

4. It is notable that applications for 16/17-year-olds under the Inherent Jurisdiction are dealt with by High Court Judges but that would not necessarily be the case if the application for the same young person was heard in the COP

The judgment went through factors which she considered marked a case as unsuitable for consideration under the streamlined/*Re X* procedure including:

1. A care order currently being in place (although the absence of one does not automatically mean that the procedure is appropriate)

2. The absence of contact with family members; this would lead to an absence of any view outside that of public bodies

3. The imminence of transition from children to adult services and any difficulties that might bring

4. Unlikely that a parent would be able to provide views on behalf of the young person and it is likely that it would be more appropriate for the parent to be a formal party or interest party in their own right

This judgment concludes with HHJ Hilder's view being that most applications in relation to young people should be brought by way of the standard procedure under a COP1.

Test to apply in the COP

Whichever procedure is used the court will then go on to consider the application. The gateway test is that there are 'reasonable grounds to believe that the young person lacks capacity'.

Once that hurdle is met the court will then go on to consider whether it should make a DOLs order. The legal test for the making of a DOLs order is the same as it is under the Inherent jurisdiction and is set out in chapter one.

Iti s worth remembering in this section that for 16 and 17-year-olds neither the local authority nor the parents/ holders of parental responsibility can consent to any deprivation and so it must be the court that approves any deprivation.

A further reminder is that DOLs orders in the COP (as well as under the Inherent Jurisdiction) are permissive, should be the least restrictive, and maintain the young person's dignity. The DOLs does not in itself place a young person in any form of placement and it does not in itself limited contact with any person. A DOLs order should, save in the case of an emergency, be obtained prior to the deprivation starting. DOLs orders in the COP are also placement specific and so a placement would have to be identified before an order could be made.

Finally it is worth reiterating that contentment on behalf of the young person to any restrictions does not dispense with the need for court approved authorisation of those deprivations. The fact that the young person lacks capacity to make a decision about DOLs is important when considering the test of consent.

Urgent applications

Just because the 'fast track' procedures cannot or are unlikely to be used in these types of cases it does not mean there is not the ability to make an urgent application for a DOLs order in relation to a young person.

One way is by making it in the first instance in the Inherent Jurisdiction to the National DOLs court by way of their urgent application list (see chapter four). Once an urgent order is made then the matter can be transferred to the COP if it is considered to be the appropriate step to take (see chapter eight).

The other option is to make an urgent application to the COP. In extremely urgent cases the DOLs team can be contacted using the details on the www.gov.uk website and a judge can be sought to give urgent directions. When the application is out of normal working hours then the call will have to be made to the Royal Courts of Justice (02079476260) and an application made to the urgent out of hours judge.

Whatever way the urgent application is made the court will want to know the following information:

1. the parties' details;

2. where the parties live;

3. the issue(s) to be decided;
4. the date of any authorisation of deprivation of liberty that has already been made;
5. the date of effective detention;
6. the parties' legal representatives;
7. any family members or others who are involved;
8. whether there have been any other court proceedings involving the parties and if so, where.
9. Whether any of the other parties have been served
10. Whether further evidence is required and if so what that is
11. Whether the young person requires representation by the OS
12. When a hearing should be fixed to hear the application fully in court hours

Summary

Although there are three ways to apply for a DOLs in the COP only two of those apply to young people and the most likely application that should be made is under the standard procedure (COP1). The tests to apply once the application is made is the same as previously considered under the Inherent Jurisdiction (set out at chapter one). It is possible to make urgent applications in relation to young people if the circumstances require it.

CHAPTER TEN

LIBERTY PROTECTION SAFEGUARDS

The Government requested that the Law Commission undertake a review of the Deprivation of Liberty Safeguards (the 'Safeguards'). This review concluded that the current process is:

1. overly technical and legalised

2. not meaningful for disabled people and their families or carers

3. fail to secure buy-in from health and social care practitioners'

As a result, the Mental Capacity (Amendment) Act 2019 sets out that the Safeguards would be replaced with new scheme called the Liberty Protection Safeguards ("LPS"). The intention was that the LPS would be more streamlined than the Safeguards, be embedded into existing care planning, and would apply to people in care homes, hospitals, supported accommodation, Shared Lives accommodation and their own homes. It is also intended that it would apply to young people for whom the Safeguards and streamlined process do not currently apply. This was said to hopefully be less distressing and intrusive for young people and their families.

There was much to-ing and fro-ing about the proposed implementation of these safeguards but on 5th April 2023, the Government announced that the implementation would be delayed "beyond the life of this Parliament".

On 18th October 2025 the government announced that it will undertake a consultation on the implementation of the LPS in the first half of 2026. The current framework and processes as set out in this guide therefore remain in place for the time being.

APPENDIX

KEY LEGAL STATUTES

This Appendix summarises the key statutory principles that govern the making of DOLs orders.

[It should be noted that the application of the tests set out in the statue and the relevant case law are set out throughout this guide and so are not specified here.]

Article 5 European Convention of Human Rights (ECHR)– Right to liberty and security

1. Everyone has the right to liberty and security of person. No one shall be deprived of his liberty save in the following cases and in accordance with a procedure prescribed by law:

    (a) the lawful detention of a person after conviction by a competent court;

    (b) the lawful arrest or detention of a person for noncompliance with the lawful order of a court or in order to secure the fulfilment of any obligation prescribed by law;

    (c) the lawful arrest or detention of a person effected for the purpose of bringing him before the competent legal authority on reasonable suspicion of having committed an offence or when it is reasonably considered necessary to prevent his committing an offence or fleeing after having done so;

(d) the detention of a minor by lawful order for the purpose of educational supervision or his lawful detention for the purpose of bringing him before the competent legal authority;

(e) the lawful detention of persons for the prevention of the spreading of infectious diseases, of persons of unsound mind, alcoholics or drug addicts or vagrants;

(f) the lawful arrest or detention of a person to prevent his effecting an unauthorised entry into the country or of a person against whom action is being taken with a view to deportation or extradition.

Article 5 Human Rights Act 1998 (HRA 1998)

The Human Rights Act 1998 incorporates the Articles of the ECHR into domestic law and this article is set out in Schedule 1 of the HRA.

Article 37 United Nations Convention on the Rights of the Child 1989 (UNCRC 1989)

States parties shall ensure that:

(a) No child shall be subjected to torture or other cruel, inhuman or degrading treatment or punishment. Neither capital punishment nor life imprisonment without possibility of release shall be imposed for offences committed by persons below eighteen years of age;

(b) No child shall be deprived of his or her liberty unlawfully or arbitrarily. The arrest, detention or imprisonment of a child shall be in conformity with the law and shall be used only as a measure of last resort and for the shortest appropriate period of time;

(c) Every child deprived of liberty shall be treated with humanity and respect for the inherent dignity of the human person, and in a manner which takes into account the needs of persons of his or her age. In particular, every child deprived of liberty shall be separated from adults unless it is considered in the child's best interest not to do so and shall have the right to maintain contact with his or her family through correspondence and visits, save in exceptional circumstances;

(d) Every child deprived of his or her liberty shall have the right to prompt access to legal and other appropriate assistance, as well as the right to challenge the legality of the deprivation of his or her liberty before a court or other competent, independent and impartial authority, and to a prompt decision on any such action.

Children Act 1989 (CA 1989)

Section 25

(1) Subject to the following provisions of this section, a child who is being looked after by a local authority in England or Wales may not be placed, and, if placed, may not be kept, in accommodation in England or Scotland provided for the purpose of restricting liberty ('secure accommodation') unless it appears –

(a) that –

(i) he has a history of absconding and is likely to abscond from any other description of accommodation; and

(ii) if he absconds, he is likely to suffer significant harm, or

(b) that if he is kept in any other description of accommodation he is likely to injure himself or other persons.

(2) The Secretary of State may by regulations –

(a) specify a maximum period –

(i) beyond which a child may not be kept in secure accommodation in England or Scotland without the authority of the court; and

(ii) for which the court may authorise a child to be kept in secure accommodation in England or Scotland;

(b) empower the court from time to time to authorise a child to be kept in secure accommodation in England or Scotland for such further period as the regulations may specify; and

(c) provide that applications to the court under this section shall be made only by local authorities in England or Wales.

(3) It shall be the duty of a court hearing an application under this section to determine whether any relevant criteria for

keeping a child in secure accommodation are satisfied in his case.

(4) If a court determines that any such criteria are satisfied, it shall make an order authorising the child to be kept in secure accommodation and specifying the maximum period for which he may be so kept.

(5) On any adjournment of the hearing of an application under this section, a court may make an interim order permitting the child to be kept during the period of the adjournment in secure accommodation.

(a) (5A) Where a local authority in England or Wales are authorised under this section to keep a child in secure accommodation in Scotland, the person in charge of the accommodation may restrict the child's liberty to the extent that the person considers appropriate, having regard to the terms of any order made by a court under this section.

(6) No court shall exercise the powers conferred by this section in respect of a child who is not legally represented in that court unless, having been informed of his right to apply for the provision of representation under Part 1 of the Legal Aid, Sentencing and Punishment of Offenders Act 2012 and having had the opportunity to do so, he refused or failed to apply.

(7) The Secretary of State may by regulations provide that –

  (a) this section shall or shall not apply to any description of children specified in the regulations;

(b) this section shall have effect in relation to children of a description specified in the regulations subject to such modifications as may be so specified;

(c) such other provisions as may be so specified shall have effect for the purpose of determining whether a child of a description specified in the regulations may be placed or kept in secure accommodation in England or Scotland;

(d) a child may only be placed in secure accommodation that is of a description specified in the regulations (and the description may in particular be framed by reference to whether the accommodation, or the person providing it, has been approved by the Secretary of State or the Scottish Ministers).

(8) The giving of an authorisation under this section shall not prejudice any power of any court in England and Wales or Scotland to give directions relating to the child to whom the authorisation relates.

(8A) Sections 168 and 169(1) to (4) of the Children's Hearings (Scotland) Act 2011 (enforcement and absconding) apply in relation to an order under subsection (4) above as they apply in relation to the orders mentioned in section 168(3) or 169(1)(a) of that Act.

(9) This section is subject to section 20(8).

Section 33 (3) (b)

(3) While a care order is in force with respect to a child, the local authority designated by the order shall –

(a) have parental responsibility for the child; and

(b) have the power (subject to the following provisions of this section) to determine the extent to which

(i) a parent, guardian or special guardian of the child; or

(ii) a person who by virtue of section 4A has parental responsibility for the child

may meet his parental responsibility for him.

(4) The authority may not exercise the power in subsection (3)(b) unless they are satisfied that it is necessary to do so in order to safeguard or promote the child's welfare.

(5) Nothing in subsection (3)(b) shall prevent a person mentioned in that provision who has care of the child from doing what is reasonable in all the circumstances of the case for the purpose of safeguarding or promoting his welfare.

Section 100

(2) No court shall exercise the High Court's inherent jurisdiction with respect to children –

(a) so as to require a child to be placed in the care, or put under the supervision, of a local authority;

(b) so as to require a child to be accommodated by or on behalf of a local authority;

(c) so as to make a child who is the subject of a care order a ward of court; or

(d) for the purpose of conferring on any local authority power to determine any question which has arisen, or which may arise, in connection with any aspect of parental responsibility for a child.

(3) No application for any exercise of the court's inherent jurisdiction with respect to children may be made by a local authority unless the authority have obtained the leave of the court.

(4) The court may only grant leave if it is satisfied that –

(a) the result which the authority wish to achieve could not be achieved through the making of any order of a kind to which subsection (5) applies; and

(b) there is reasonable cause to believe that if the court's inherent jurisdiction is not exercised with respect to the child he is likely to suffer significant harm.

(5) This subsection applies to any order –

(a) made otherwise than in the exercise of the court's inherent jurisdiction; and

(b) which the local authority is entitled to apply for (assuming, in the case of any application which may only be made with leave, that leave is granted).

Mental Capacity Act 2005 (MCA)

Section 1

The principles

(1) ....

(2) A person must be assumed to have capacity unless it is established that he lacks capacity.

(3) A person is not to be treated as unable to make a decision unless all practicable steps to help him to do so have been taken without success.

(4) A person is not to be treated as unable to make a decision merely because he makes an unwise decision.

(5) An act done, or decision made, under this Act for or on behalf of a person who lacks capacity must be done, or made, in his best interests.

(6) Before the act is done, or the decision is made, regard must be had to whether the purpose for which it is needed can be as effectively achieved in a way that is less restrictive of the person's rights and freedom of action.

Section 2:

People who lack capacity

(1) For the purposes of this Act, a person lacks capacity in relation to a matter if at the material time he is unable to make a decision for himself in relation to the matter because of an impairment of, or a disturbance in the functioning of, the mind or brain.

(2) It does not matter whether the impairment or disturbance is permanent or temporary.

(3) A lack of capacity cannot be established merely by reference to—

(a) a person's age or appearance, or

(b) a condition of his, or an aspect of his behaviour, which might lead others to make unjustified assumptions about his capacity.

(4) In proceedings under this Act or any other enactment, any question whether a person lacks capacity within the meaning of this Act must be decided on the balance of probabilities.

Section 3

Inability to make decisions

(1) For the purposes of section 2, a person is unable to make a decision for himself if he is unable—

(a) to understand the information relevant to the decision,

(b) to retain that information,

(c) to use or weigh that information as part of the process of making the decision, or

(d) to communicate his decision (whether by talking, using sign language or any other means).

(2) A person is not to be regarded as unable to understand the information relevant to a decision if he is able to understand an explanation of it given to him in a way that is appropriate to his circumstances (using simple language, visual aids or any other means).

(3) The fact that a person is able to retain the information relevant to a decision for a short period only does not prevent him from being regarded as able to make the decision.

(4) The information relevant to a decision includes information about the reasonably foreseeable consequences of—

(a) deciding one way or another, or

(b) failing to make the decision.

4A Restriction on deprivation of liberty

(1) This Act does not authorise any person ("D") to deprive any other person ("P") of his liberty.

(2) But that is subject to—

(a) the following provisions of this section, and

(b) section 4B.

(3) D may deprive P of his liberty if, by doing so, D is giving effect to a relevant decision of the court.

(4) A relevant decision of the court is a decision made by an order under section 16(2)(a) in relation to a matter concerning P's personal welfare.

(5) D may deprive P of his liberty if the deprivation is authorised by Schedule A1 (hospital and care home residents: deprivation of liberty).

(6) D may deprive P of liberty if, by doing so, D is carrying out arrangements authorised under Schedule AA1 (arrangements enabling the care and treatment of persons who lack capacity).

5 Acts in connection with care or treatment

(1) If a person ("D") does an act in connection with the care or treatment of another person ("P"), the act is one to which this section applies if—

(a) before doing the act, D takes reasonable steps to establish whether P lacks capacity in relation to the matter in question, and

(b) when doing the act, D reasonably believes—

(i) that P lacks capacity in relation to the matter, and

(ii) that it will be in P's best interests for the act to be done.

(2) D does not incur any liability in relation to the act that he would not have incurred if P—

(a) had had capacity to consent in relation to the matter, and

(b) had consented to D's doing the act.

(3) Nothing in this section excludes a person's civil liability for loss or damage, or his criminal liability, resulting from his negligence in doing the act.

(4) Nothing in this section affects the operation of sections 24 to 26 (advance decisions to refuse treatment).

Section 16

Power to make decisions and appoint deputies on behalf of P in respect of their personal welfare or property and affairs.

(1) This section applies if a person ("P") lacks capacity in relation to a matter or matters concerning—

(a) P's personal welfare, or

(b) P's property and affairs.

(2) The court may—

(a) by making an order, make the decision or decisions on P's behalf in relation to the matter or matters, or

(b) appoint a person (a "deputy") to make decisions on P's behalf in relation to the matter or matters.

Section 48

Interim orders and directions

The court may, pending the determination of an application to it in relation to a person ("P"), make an order or give directions in respect of any matter if—

(a) there is reason to believe that P lacks capacity in relation to the matter,

(b) the matter is one to which its powers under this Act extend, and

(c) it is in P's best interests to make the order, or give the directions, without delay.

Part 11 – Deprivation of liberty

The practice direction to this Part sets out procedure governing –

(a) applications to the court for orders relating to the deprivation, or proposed deprivation, of liberty of P; and

(b) proceedings (for example, relating to costs or appeals) connected with or consequent on such applications.

The Mental Capacity Act 2005 (Transfer of Proceedings) Order 2007

Article 2

Transfers from the Court of Protection to a court having jurisdiction under the Children Act

(1) This article applies to any proceedings in the Court of Protection which relate to a person under 18.

(2) The Court of Protection may direct the transfer of the whole or part of the proceedings to a court having jurisdiction under the Children Act where it considers that in all the circumstances, it is just and convenient to transfer the proceedings.

(3) In making a determination, the Court of Protection must have regard to—

- (a) whether the proceedings should be heard together with other proceedings that are pending in a court having jurisdiction under the Children Act;
- (b) whether any order that may be made by a court having jurisdiction under that Act is likely to be a more appropriate way of dealing with the proceedings;
- (c) the need to meet any requirements that would apply if the proceedings had been started in a court having jurisdiction under the Children Act; and
- (d) any other matter that the court considers relevant.

(4) The Court of Protection—

(a) may exercise the power to make an order under paragraph (2) on an application or on its own initiative; and

(b) where it orders a transfer, must give reasons for its decision.

(5) Any proceedings transferred under this article—

(a) are to be treated for all purposes as if they were proceedings under the Children Act which had been started in a court having jurisdiction under that Act; and

(b) are to be dealt with after the transfer in accordance with directions given by a court having jurisdiction under that Act.

Article 3

Transfers from a court having jurisdiction under the Children Act to the Court of Protection

(1) This article applies to any proceedings in a court having jurisdiction under the Children Act which relate to a person under 18.

(2) A court having jurisdiction under the Children Act may direct the transfer of the whole or part of the proceedings to the Court of Protection where it considers that in all circumstances, it is just and convenient to transfer the proceedings.

(3) In making a determination, the court having jurisdiction under the Children Act must have regard to—

(a) whether the proceedings should be heard together with other proceedings that are pending in the Court of Protection;

(b) whether any order that may be made by the Court of Protection is likely to be a more appropriate way of dealing with the proceedings;

(c) the extent to which any order made as respects a person who lacks capacity is likely to continue to have effect when that person reaches 18; and

(d) any other matter that the court considers relevant.

(4) A court having jurisdiction under the Children Act—

(a) may exercise the power to make an order under paragraph (2) on an application or on its own initiative; and

(b) where it orders a transfer, must give reasons for its decision.

(5) Any proceedings transferred under this article—(a)are to be treated for all purposes as if they were proceedings under the Mental Capacity Act 2005 which had been started in the Court of Protection; and

(b) are to be dealt with after the transfer in accordance with directions given by the Court of Protection.

MORE BOOKS BY LAW BRIEF PUBLISHING

A selection of our other titles available now:-

'A Practical Guide to Probation Breaches and Other Applications' by Mark Thomas
'A Practical Guide to Remarriage and Divorce' by Cordelia Williams & Claire Howard
'A Practical Guide to Privacy, Transparency, Reporting Restrictions and Closed Proceedings in the Court of Protection' by Laura Mannering
'Beaumont on Barristers – A Guide to Defending Disciplinary Proceedings (Second Edition)' by Marc Beaumont
'A Practical Guide to Payments for Environmental Services' by Ben Sharples
'A Practical Guide to the Law of Pregnancy and Maternity at Work' by Rebecca Thomas
'A Practical Guide to Redundancy – Second Edition' by Philip Hyland & Collette Moore
'A Practical Guide to International Issues for Scottish Family Lawyers' by Susie Mountain, Donna McKay, Ken MacDonald
'A Practical Guide to the Law on Deprivation of Liberty' by Ben Troke
'A Practical Guide to Rights over Airspace and Subsoil – Second Edition' by Daniel Gatty
'A Practical Guide to the Law in Relation to Inquests' by Ramya Nagesh
'A Practical Guide to the Construction and Rectification of Wills and Trust Instruments (Second Edition)' by Edward Hewitt
'A Practical Guide to Data Protection in Social Housing' by Clare Paterson
'A Practical Guide to Spousal Maintenance – Second Edition' by Liz Cowell
'A Practical Guide to International Parental Child Abduction Law (England and Wales)' by Dr Onyója Momoh
'A Practical Guide to Deprivation of British Citizenship' by Sean Ell
'A Practical Guide to Commercial Property Service Charges' by Rachel Garton
'A Practical Guide to Clinical Negligence – Third Edition' by Geoffrey Simpson-Scott (Geoff)
'A Practical Guide to the Rights of Grandparents in Children Proceedings – Second Edition' by Stuart Barlow

'The Electronic Communications Code: A Practical Guide – Second Edition' by Kerry Bretherton KC, James Castle, Mark Loveday
'A Practical Guide to the Independent School Standards – September 2023 Edition' by Sarah McKimm
'A Practical Guide to Estate Administration and Crypto Assets' by Richard Marshall
'A Practical Guide to Parental Alienation in Private and Public Law Children Cases' by Sam King QC & Frankie Shama
'Contested Heritage – Removing Art from Land and Historic Buildings' by Richard Harwood QC, Catherine Dobson, David Sawtell
'The Limits of Separate Legal Personality: When Those Running a Company Can Be Held Personally Liable for Losses Caused to Third Parties Outside of the Company' by Dr Mike Wilkinson
'A Practical Guide to Transgender Law' by Robin Moira White & Nicola Newbegin
'A Practical Guide to 'Stranded Spouses' in Family Law' by Mani Singh Basi
'A Practical Guide to Residential Freehold Conveyancing' by Lorraine Richardson
'A Practical Guide to Pensions on Divorce for Lawyers' by Bryan Scant
'A Practical Guide to Challenging Sham Marriage Allegations in Immigration Law' by Priya Solanki
'A Practical Guide to Digital Communications Evidence in Criminal Law' by Sam Willis
'A Practical Guide to Legal Rights in Scotland' by Sarah-Jane Macdonald
'A Practical Guide to New Build Conveyancing' by Paul Sams & Rebecca East
'A Practical Guide to Inherited Wealth on Divorce' by Hayley Trim
'A Practical Guide to Practice Direction 12J and Domestic Abuse in Private Law Children Proceedings' by Rebecca Cross & Malvika Jaganmohan
'A Practical Guide to Confiscation and Restraint' by Narita Bahra QC, John Carl Townsend, David Winch
'A Practical Guide to the Law of Forests in Scotland' by Philip Buchan
'A Practical Guide to Health and Medical Cases in Immigration Law' by Rebecca Chapman & Miranda Butler
'A Practical Guide to Bad Character Evidence for Criminal Practitioners by Aparna Rao
'A Practical Guide to Extradition Law post-Brexit' by Myles Grandison et al
'A Practical Guide to Hoarding and Mental Health for Housing Lawyers' by Rachel Coyle

'Stephens on Contractual Indemnities' by Richard Stephens
'A Practical Guide to the EU Succession Regulation' by Richard Frimston
'A Practical Guide to Solicitor and Client Costs – Second Edition' by Robin Dunne
'Constructive Dismissal – Practice Pointers and Principles' by Benjimin Burgher
'A Practical Guide to Religion and Belief Discrimination Claims in the Workplace' by Kashif Ali
'A Practical Guide to the Law of Medical Treatment Decisions' by Ben Troke
'Fundamental Dishonesty and QOCS in Personal Injury Proceedings: Law and Practice' by Jake Rowley
'A Practical Guide to the Law in Relation to School Exclusions' by Charlotte Hadfield & Alice de Coverley
'A Practical Guide to Divorce for the Silver Separators' by Karin Walker
'The Right to be Forgotten – The Law and Practical Issues' by Melissa Stock
'A Practical Guide to Planning Law and Rights of Way in National Parks, the Broads and AONBs' by James Maurici QC, James Neill et al
'A Practical Guide to Election Law' by Tom Tabori
'A Practical Guide to the Law in Relation to Surrogacy' by Andrew Powell
'A Practical Guide to Claims Arising from Fatal Accidents – Second Edition' by James Patience
'A Practical Guide to Asbestos Claims' by Jonathan Owen & Gareth McAloon
'A Practical Guide to Stamp Duty Land Tax in England and Northern Ireland' by Suzanne O'Hara
'A Practical Guide to the Law of Farming Partnerships' by Philip Whitcomb
'A Practical Guide to the Law of Unlawful Eviction and Harassment – Second Edition' by Stephanie Lovegrove
'A Practical Guide to Costs in Personal Injury Claims – Second Edition' by Matthew Hoe
'A Practical Guide to the General Data Protection Regulation (GDPR) – Second Edition' by Keith Markham
'A Practical Guide to Working with Litigants in Person and McKenzie Friends in Family Cases' by Stuart Barlow
'Protecting Unregistered Brands: A Practical Guide to the Law of Passing Off' by Lorna Brazell
'A Practical Guide to Secondary Liability and Joint Enterprise Post-Jogee' by Joanne Cecil & James Mehigan

'A Practical Guide to the Pre-Action RTA Claims Protocol for Personal Injury Lawyers' by Antonia Ford

'A Practical Guide to Neighbour Disputes and the Law' by Alexander Walsh

'A Practical Guide to Coercive Control for Legal Practitioners and Victims' by Rachel Horman

'A Practical Guide to the Law of Driverless Cars – Second Edition'

by Alex Glassbrook, Emma Northey & Scarlett Milligan

'A Practical Guide to TOLATA Claims' by Greg Williams

'A Practical Guide to Elderly Law – Second Edition' by Justin Patten

'A Practical Guide to Responding to Housing Disrepair and Unfitness Claims' by Iain Wightwick

'A Practical Guide to the Law of Bullying and Harassment in the Workplace' by Philip Hyland

'How to Be a Freelance Solicitor: A Practical Guide to the SRA-Regulated Freelance Solicitor Model' by Paul Bennett

'A Practical Guide to Prison Injury Claims' by Malcolm Johnson

'A Practical Guide to Advising Clients at the Police Station' by Colin Stephen McKeown-Beaumont

'A Practical Guide to Antisocial Behaviour Injunctions – Second Edition' by Iain Wightwick

'Practical Mediation: A Guide for Mediators, Advocates, Advisers, Lawyers, and Students in Civil, Commercial, Business, Property, Workplace, and Employment Cases' by Jonathan Dingle with John Sephton

'The Mini-Pupillage Workbook' by David Boyle

'A Practical Guide to Crofting Law' by Brian Inkster

'A Practical Guide to the Law of Domain Names and Cybersquatting' by Andrew Clemson

'A Practical Guide to the Law of Gender Pay Gap Reporting' by Harini Iyengar

'NHS Whistleblowing and the Law' by Joseph England

'Employment Law and the Gig Economy' by Nigel Mackay & Annie Powell

'A Practical Guide to Noise Induced Hearing Loss (NIHL) Claims' by Andrew Mckie, Ian Skeate, Gareth McAloon

'An Introduction to Beauty Negligence Claims – A Practical Guide for the Personal Injury Practitioner' by Greg Almond

'Intercompany Agreements for Transfer Pricing Compliance' by Paul Sutton

'Zen and the Art of Mediation' by Martin Plowman

'A Practical Guide to Adoption for Family Lawyers' by Graham Pegg

'A Practical Guide to Industrial Disease Claims' by Andrew Mckie & Ian Skeate
'A Practical Guide to Conducting a Sheriff Court Proof' by Andrew Stevenson
'A Practical Guide to Vicarious Liability' by Mariel Irvine
'A Practical Guide to Applications for Landlord's Consent and Variation of Leases' by Mark Shelton
'A Practical Guide to Relief from Sanctions Post-Mitchell and Denton' by Peter Causton
'A Practical Guide to Equity Release for Advisors' by Paul Sams
'A Practical Guide to Financial Services Claims' by Chris Hegarty
'A Practical Guide to Financial Ombudsman Service Claims' by Adam Temple & Robert Scrivenor
'A Practical Guide to Running Housing Disrepair and Cavity Wall Claims – Second Edition' by Andrew Mckie & Ian Skeate
'A Practical Guide to Holiday Sickness Claims – Second Edition' by Andrew Mckie & Ian Skeate
'Arguments and Tactics for Personal Injury and Clinical Negligence Claims' by Dorian Williams
'A Practical Guide to Drone Law' by Rufus Ballaster, Andrew Firman, Eleanor Clot
'On Experts: CPR35 for Lawyers and Experts' by David Boyle
'An Introduction to Personal Injury Law' by David Boyle

These books and more are available to order online direct from the publisher at www.lawbriefpublishing.com, where you can also read free sample chapters. For any queries, call us on 0844 587 2383 or email us at mail@lawbriefpublishing.com.

Our books are all generally in stock at www.amazon.co.uk with free next day delivery for Prime members, and at good legal bookshops such as Wildy & Sons.

We are regularly launching new books in our series of practical day-to-day practitioners' guides. Visit our website and join our free newsletter to be kept informed and to receive special offers, free chapters, etc.

You can also follow us on Twitter at www.twitter.com/lawbriefpub.

www.ingramcontent.com/pod-product-compliance
Lightning Source LLC
LaVergne TN
LVHW022109200926
848481LV00003B/1125